WHY I AM NOT GOING TO BUY A COMPUTER

Why I Am Not Going to Buy a Computer

ESSAYS

Wendell Berry

COUNTERPOINT
Berkeley, California

COUNTERPOINTS 6

ISBN: 978-1-64009-457-4

The Library of Congress Cataloging-in-Publication Data is available.

Series design by Jenny Carrow
Cover design by Lexi Earle
Book design by Jordan Koluch

COUNTERPOINT
2560 Ninth Street, Suite 318
Berkeley, CA 94710
www.counterpointpress.com

Printed in the United States of America

10 9 8 7 6 5 4 3 2

Contents

WHY I AM NOT GOING TO BUY A COMPUTER

Like almost everybody else, I am hooked to the energy corporations, which I do not admire. I hope to become less hooked to them. In my work, I try to be as little hooked to them as possible. As a farmer, I do almost all of my work with horses. As a writer, I work with a pencil or a pen and a piece of paper.

My wife types my work on a Royal standard typewriter bought new in 1956 and as good now as it was then. As she types, she sees things that are wrong and marks them with small checks in the margins. She is my best critic because she is the one most familiar with my habitual errors and weaknesses. She also understands, sometimes better than I do, what *ought* to be said. We have, I think, a literary cottage industry that works well and pleasantly. I do not see anything wrong with it.

A number of people, by now, have told me that I could greatly improve things by buying a computer. My answer is that I am not going to do it. I have several reasons, and they are good ones.

The first is the one I mentioned at the beginning. I would hate to think that my work as a writer could not be done without a direct dependence on strip-mined coal. How could I write conscientiously against the rape of nature if I were, in the act of writing, implicated in the rape? For the same reason, it matters to me that my writing is done in the daytime, without electric light.

I do not admire the computer manufacturers a great deal more than I admire the energy industries. I have seen their advertisements, attempting to seduce struggling or failing farmers into the belief that they can solve their problems by buying yet another piece of expensive equipment. I am familiar with their propaganda campaigns that have put computers into public schools in need of books. That computers are expected to become as common as TV sets in 'the future' does not impress me or matter to me. I do not own a TV set. I do not see that computers are bringing us one step nearer to anything that does matter to me: peace, economic justice, ecological health, political honesty, family and community stability, good work.

What would a computer cost me? More

money, for one thing, than I can afford, and more than I wish to pay to people whom I do not admire. But the cost would not be just monetary. It is well understood that technological innovation always requires the discarding of the 'old model' – the 'old model' in this case being not just our old Royal standard, but my wife, my critic, my closest reader, my fellow worker. Thus (and I think this is typical of present-day technological innovation), what would be superseded would be not only something, but somebody. In order to be technologically up-to-date as a writer, I would have to sacrifice an association that I am dependent upon and that I treasure.

My final and perhaps my best reason for not owning a computer is that I do not wish to fool myself. I disbelieve, and therefore strongly resent, the assertion that I or anybody else could write better or more easily with a computer than with a pencil. I do not see why I should not be as scientific about this as the next fellow: when somebody has used a computer to write work that is demonstrably better than Dante's, and when this better is demonstrably attributable to the use of a computer, then I will speak of computers with a more respectful tone of voice, though I still will not buy one.

To make myself as plain as I can, I should give my standards for technological innovation in my own work. They are as follows:

1. The new tool should be cheaper than the one it replaces.
2. It should be at least as small in scale as the one it replaces.
3. It should do work that is clearly and demonstrably better than the one it replaces.

4. It should use less energy than the one it replaces.
5. If possible, it should use some form of solar energy, such as that of the body.
6. It should be repairable by a person of ordinary intelligence, provided that he or she has the necessary tools.
7. It should be purchasable and repairable as near to home as possible.
8. It should come from a small, privately owned shop or store that will take it back for maintenance and repair.
9. It should not replace or disrupt anything good that already exists, and this includes family and community relationships.

AFTER THE FOREGOING essay, first published in the *New England Review and*

Bread Loaf Quarterly, was reprinted in *Harper's*, the *Harper's* editors published the following letters in response and permitted me a reply.   W. B.

LETTERS

Wendell Berry provides writers enslaved by the computer with a handy alternative: Wife – a low-tech energy-saving device. Drop a pile of handwritten notes on Wife and you get back a finished manuscript, edited while it was typed. What computer can do that? Wife meets all of Berry's uncompromising standards for technological innovation: she's cheap, repairable near home, and good for the family structure. Best of all, Wife is politically correct because she breaks a writer's 'direct dependence on strip-mined coal.'

History teaches us that Wife can also be used to beat rugs and wash clothes by hand, thus eliminating the need for the vacuum cleaner and washing machine, two more nasty machines that threaten the act of writing.

Gordon Inkeles
Miranda, Calif.

I have no quarrel with Berry because he prefers to write with pencil and paper; that is his choice. But he implies that I and others are somehow impure because we choose to write on a computer. I do not admire the energy corporations, either. Their shortcoming is not that they produce electricity but how they go about it. They are poorly managed because they are blind to long-term consequences. To solve this problem, wouldn't it make more sense to correct the precise error they are making rather than simply ignore their product? I would be happy to join Berry in a protest against strip mining, but I intend to keep plugging this computer into the wall with a clear conscience.

James Rhoads
Battle Creek, Mich.

I enjoyed reading Berry's declaration of intent never to buy a personal computer in the same way that I enjoy reading about the belief systems of unfamiliar tribal cultures. I tried to imagine a tool that would meet Berry's criteria for superiority to his old manual typewriter. The clear winner is the quill pen. It is cheaper, smaller, more energy-efficient, human-powered, easily repaired, and non-disruptive of existing relationships.

Berry also requires that this tool must be 'clearly and demonstrably better' than the one it replaces. But surely we all recognize by now that 'better' is in the mind of the beholder. To the quill pen aficionado, the benefits obtained from elegant calligraphy might well outweigh all others.

I have no particular desire to see Berry use a word processor; if he doesn't like computers, that's fine with me. However, I do object to his portrayal of this reluctance as a moral virtue. Many of us have found that computers can be an invaluable tool in the fight to protect our environment. In addition to helping me write, my personal computer gives me access to up-to-the-minute reports on the workings of the EPA and the nuclear industry. I participate in electronic bulletin boards

*on which environmental activists dis-
cuss strategy and warn each other
about urgent legislative issues. Perhaps
Berry feels that the Sierra Club should
eschew modern printing technology,
which is highly wasteful of energy, in
favor of having its members hand-copy
the club's magazines and other mail-
ings each month?*

*Nathaniel S. Borenstein
Pittsburgh, Pa.*

*The value of a computer to a writer is
that it is a tool not for generating ideas
but for typing and editing words. It is
cheaper than a secretary (or a wife!)
and arguably more fuel-efficient. And
it enables spouses who are not inclined
to provide free labor more time to con-
centrate on their own work.*

We should support alternatives

both to coal-generated electricity and to IBM-style technocracy. But I am reluctant to entertain alternatives that presuppose the traditional subservience of one class to another. Let the PCs come and the wives and servants go seek more meaningful work.

Toby Koosman
Knoxville, Tenn.

Berry asks how he could write conscientiously against the rape of nature if in the act of writing on a computer he was implicated in the rape. I find it ironic that a writer who sees the underlying connectedness of things would allow his diatribe against computers to be published in a magazine that carries ads for the National Rural Electric Co-operative Association, Marlboro, Phillips Petroleum, McDonnell Douglas, and yes, even Smith-Corona. If Berry rests comfortably at night, he must be using sleeping pills.

Bradley C. Johnson
Grand Forks, N.D.

Wendell Berry Replies

THE FOREGOING LETTERS surprised me with the intensity of the feelings they expressed. According to the writers' testimony, there is nothing wrong with their computers; they are utterly satisfied with them and all that they stand for. My correspondents are certain that I am wrong and that I am, moreover, on the losing side, a side already relegated to the dustbin of history. And yet they grow huffy and condescending over my tiny dissent. What are they so anxious about?

I can only conclude that I have scratched

the skin of a technological fundamentalism that, like other fundamentalisms, wishes to monopolize a whole society and, therefore, cannot tolerate the smallest difference of opinion. At the slightest hint of a threat to their complacency, they repeat, like a chorus of toads, the notes sounded by their leaders in industry. The past was gloomy, drudgery-ridden, servile, meaningless, and slow. The present, thanks only to purchasable products, is meaningful, bright, lively, centralized, and fast. The future, thanks only to more purchasable products, is going to be even better. Thus consumers become salesmen, and the world is made safer for corporations.

I am also surprised by the meanness with which two of these writers refer to my wife. In order to imply that I am a tyrant, they suggest by both direct statement and innuendo that she is subservient, characterless, and stupid – a mere 'device' easily forced to provide meaningless 'free labor.' I understand that it is impossible to make an adequate public defense of one's private life and so I will only point out that there are a number of kinder possibilities that my critics have disdained to imagine: that my wife may do this work because she wants to and likes to; that she may find some use and some meaning in it; that she may not work for nothing. These gentlemen obviously think themselves feminists of the most correct and principled sort, and yet they do not hesitate to stereotype and in-sult, on the basis of one fact, a woman they do not know. They are audacious and irre-sponsible gossips.

In his letter, Bradley C. Johnson rushes past the possibility of sense in what I said in my essay by implying that I am or ought to be a fanatic. That I am a person of this century and am implicated in many practices that I regret is fully acknowledged at the beginning of my essay. I did not say that I proposed to end forthwith all my involvement in harmful technology, for I do not know how to do that. I said merely that I want to limit such involvement, and to a certain extent I do know how to do that. If some technology does damage to the world – as two of the above letters seem to agree that it does – then why is it not reasonable, and indeed moral, to try to limit one's use of that technology? *Of course*, I think that I am right to do this.

I would not think so, obviously, if I agreed with Nathaniel S. Borenstein that '"better" is in the mind of the beholder.' But if he truly believes this, I do not see why he bothers with his personal computer's 'up-to-the-minute reports on the workings of the EPA and the nuclear industry' or why he wishes to be warned about 'urgent legislative issues.' According to his system, the 'better' in a bureaucratic, industrial, or legislative mind is as good as the 'better' in his. His mind apparently is being subverted by an objective standard of some sort, and he had better look out.

Borenstein does not say what he does after his computer has drummed him awake. I assume from his letter that he must send donations to conservation organizations and letters to officials. Like James Rhoads, at any rate, he has a clear conscience. But this is what is wrong with the conservation movement. It has a clear conscience. The guilty are always other people, and the wrong is always somewhere else. That is why Borenstein finds his 'electronic bulletin board' so handy. To the conservation movement, it is only production that causes environmental degradation; the consumption that supports the production is rarely acknowledged to be at fault. The ideal of the run-of-the-mill conservationist is to impose restraints upon production without limiting consumption or burdening the consciences of consumers.

But virtually all of our consumption now is extravagant, and virtually all of it consumes the world. It is not beside the point that most electrical power comes from strip-mined coal. The history of the exploitation of the Appalachian coal fields is long, and it is available to readers. I do not see how anyone can read it and plug in any appliance with a clear conscience. If Rhoads can do so, that does not mean that his conscience is clear; it means that his conscience is not working.

To the extent that we consume, in our present circumstances, we are guilty. To the extent that we guilty consumers are conservationists, we are absurd. But what can we do? Must we go on writing letters to politicians and donating to conservation organizations until the majority of our fellow citizens agree with us? Or can we do something directly to solve our share of the problem?

I am a conservationist. I believe wholeheartedly in putting pressure on the politicians and in maintaining the conservation organizations. But I wrote my little essay partly in distrust of centralization. I don't think that the government and the conservation organizations alone will ever make us a conserving society. Why do I need a centralized computer system to alert me to environmental crises? That I live every hour of every day in an environmental crisis I know from all my senses. Why then is not my first duty to reduce, so far as I can, my own consumption?

Finally, it seems to me that none of my correspondents recognizes the innovativeness of my essay. If the use of a computer is a new idea, then a newer idea is not to use one.

(1987)

FEMINISM, THE BODY, AND THE MACHINE

S ome time ago *Harper's* reprinted a short essay of mine in which I gave some of my reasons for refusing to buy a computer. Until that time, the vast numbers of people who disagree with my writings had mostly ignored them. An unusual number of people, however, neglected to ignore my insensitivity to the wonders of computer enhancement. Some of us, it seems, would be better off if we would just realize that this is already the best of all possible worlds, and is going to get even better if we will just buy the right equipment.

Harper's published only five of the letters the editors received in response to my essay, and they published only negative letters. But of the twenty letters received by the *Harper's* editors, who forwarded copies to me, three were favorable. This I look upon as extremely gratifying. If these letters may be taken as a fair sample, then one in seven of *Harper's* readers agreed with me. If I had guessed beforehand, I would have guessed that my supporters would have been fewer than one in a thousand. And so I suppose, after further reflection, that my surprise at the intensity of the attacks on me is mistaken. There are more of us than I thought. Maybe there is even a 'significant number' of us.

Only one of the negative letters seemed to me to have much intelligence in it. That one was from R. N. Neff of Arlington, Virginia, who scored a direct hit: 'Not to be obtuse, but being willing to bare my illiterate soul for all to see, is there indeed a "work demonstrably better than Dante's" . . . which was written on a Royal standard typewriter?' I like this retort so well that I am tempted to count it a favorable response, raising the total to four. The rest of the negative replies, like the five published ones, were more feeling than intelligent. Some of them, indeed, might be fairly described as exclamatory.

One of the letter writers described me as 'a fool' and 'doubly a fool,' but fortunately misspelled my name, leaving me a speck of hope that I am not the 'Wendell Barry' he was talking about. Two others accused me of self-righteousness, by which they seem to have meant that they think they are righter than I think I am. And another accused me of being more concerned about my own moral purity than with 'any ecological effect,' thereby making the sort of razor-sharp philosophical distinction that could cause a person to be elected president.

But most of my attackers deal in feelings either feminist or technological, or both. The feelings expressed seem to be representative of what the state of public feeling currently permits to be felt, and of what public rhetoric currently permits to be said. The feelings, that is, are similar enough, from one letter to another, to be thought representative, and as representative letters they have an interest greater than the quarrel that occasioned them.

WITHOUT EXCEPTION, THE feminist letters accuse me of exploiting my wife, and they do not scruple to allow the most insulting implications of their indictment to fall upon my wife. They fail entirely to see that my essay does not give any support to their accusation – or if they see it, they do not care. My essay, in fact, does not characterize my wife beyond saying that she types my manuscripts and tells me what she thinks about them. It does not say what her motives are, how much work she does, or whether or how she is paid. Aside from saying that she is my wife and that I value the help she gives me with my work, it says nothing about our marriage. It says nothing about our economy.

There is no way, then, to escape the conclusion that my wife and I are subjected in these letters to a condemnation by category. My offense is that I am a man who receives some help from his wife; my wife's offense is that she is a woman who does some work for her husband – which work, according to her critics and mine, makes her a drudge, exploited by a conventional subservience.

And my detractors have, as I say, no evidence to support any of this. Their accusation rests on a syllogism of the flimsiest sort: my wife helps me in my work, some wives who have helped their husbands in their work have been exploited, therefore my wife is exploited.

This, of course, outrages justice to about the same extent that it insults intelligence. Any respectable system of justice exists in part as a protection against such accusations. In a just society nobody is expected to plead guilty to a general indictment, because in a just society nobody can be convicted on a general indictment. What is required for a just conviction is a particular accusation that can be *proved*. My accusers have made no such accusation against me.

THAT FEMINISTS OR any other advocates of human liberty and dignity should resort to insult and injustice is regrettable. It is equally regrettable that all of the feminist attacks on my essay implicitly deny the validity of two decent and probably necessary possibilities: marriage as a state of mutual help, and the household as an economy.

Marriage, in what is evidently its most popular version, is now on the one hand an intimate 'relationship' involving (ideally) two successful careerists in the same bed, and on the other hand a sort of private political system in which rights and interests must be constantly asserted and defended. Marriage, in other words, has now taken the form of divorce: a prolonged and impassioned negotiation as to how things shall be divided. During their understandably temporary association, the 'married' couple will typically consume a large quantity of merchandise and a large portion of each other.

The modern household is the place where the consumptive couple do their consuming. Nothing productive is done there. Such work as is done there is done at the expense of the resident couple or family, and to the profit of suppliers of energy and household technology. For entertainment, the inmates consume television or purchase other consumable diversion elsewhere.

There are, however, still some married couples who understand themselves as belonging to their marriage, to each other, and to their children. What they have they have in common, and so, to them, helping each other does not seem merely to damage their ability to compete against each other. To them, 'mine' is not so powerful or necessary a pronoun as 'ours.'

This sort of marriage usually has at its heart a household that is to some extent productive. The couple, that is, makes around itself a household economy that involves the work of both wife and husband, that gives them a measure of economic independence and self-protection, a measure of self-employment, a measure of freedom, as well as a common ground and a common satisfaction. Such a household economy may employ the disciplines and skills of housewifery, of carpentry and other trades of building and maintenance, of gardening and other branches of subsistence agriculture, and even of woodlot management and wood-cutting. It may also involve a 'cottage industry' of some kind, such as a small literary enterprise.

It is obvious how much skill and industry either partner may put into such a household and what a good economic result such work may have, and yet it is a kind of work now frequently held in contempt. Men in general were the first to hold it in contempt as they departed from it for the sake of the professional salary or the hourly wage, and now it is held in contempt by such feminists as those who attacked my essay. Thus farm wives who help to run the kind of household economy that I have described are apt to be asked by feminists, and with great condescension, 'But what do you *do*?' By this they invariably mean that there is something better to do than to make one's marriage and household, and by better they invariably mean 'employment outside the home.'

I KNOW THAT I am in dangerous territory, and so I had better be plain: what I have to say about marriage and household I mean to apply to men as much as to women. I do not believe that there is anything better to do than to make one's marriage and household, whether one is a man or a woman.

I do not believe that 'employment outside the home' is as valuable or important or satisfying as employment at home, for either men or women. It is clear to me from my experience as a teacher, for example, that children need an ordinary daily association with *both* parents. They need to see their parents at work; they need, at first, to play at the work they see their parents doing, and then they need to work with their parents. It does not matter so much that this working together should be what is called 'quality time,' but it matters a great deal that the work done should have the dignity of economic value.

I should say too that I understand how fortunate I have been in being able to do an appreciable part of my work at home. I know that in many marriages both husband and wife are now finding it necessary to work away from home. This issue, of course, is troubled by the question of what is meant by 'necessary,' but it is true that a family living that not so long ago was ordinarily supplied by one job now routinely requires two or more. My interest is not to quarrel with individuals, men or women, who work away from home, but rather to ask why we should consider this general working away from home to be a desirable state of things, either for people or for marriage, for our society or for our country.

If I had written in my essay that my wife worked as a typist and editor for a publisher, doing the same work that she does for me, no feminists, I daresay, would have written to *Harper's* to attack me for exploiting her – even though, for all they knew, I might have forced her to do such work in order to keep me in gambling money. It would have been assumed as a matter of course that if she had a job away from home she was a 'liberated woman,' possessed of a dignity that no home could confer upon her.

As I have said before, I understand that one cannot construct an adequate public defense of a private life. Anything that I might say here about my marriage would be immediately (and rightly) suspect on the ground that it would be only *my* testimony. But for the sake of argument, let us suppose that whatever work my wife does, as a member of our marriage and household, she does both as a full economic partner and as her own boss, and let us suppose that the economy we have is adequate to our needs. Why, granting that supposition, should anyone assume that my wife would increase her freedom or dignity or satisfaction by becoming the employee of a boss, who would be in turn also a corporate underling and in no sense a partner?

Why would any woman who would

refuse, properly, to take the marital vow of obedience (on the ground, presumably, that subservience to a mere human being is beneath human dignity) then regard as 'liberating' a job that puts her under the authority of a boss (man or woman) whose authority specifically requires and expects obedience? It is easy enough to see why women came to object to the role of Blondie, a mostly decorative custodian of a degraded, consumptive modern household, preoccupied with clothes, shopping, gossip, and outwitting her husband. But are we to assume that one may fittingly cease to be Blondie by becoming Dagwood? Is the life of a corporate underling – even acknowledging that corporate underlings are well paid – an acceptable end to our quest for human dignity and worth? It is clear enough by now that one does not cease to be an underling by reaching 'the top.' Corporate life is composed only of lower underlings and higher underlings. Bosses are everywhere, and all the bosses are underlings. This is invariably revealed when the time comes for accepting responsibility for something unpleasant, such as the Exxon fiasco in Prince William Sound, for which certain lower underlings are blamed but no higher underling is responsible. The underlings at the top, like telephone operators, have authority and power, but no responsibility.

And the oppressiveness of some of this office work defies belief. Edward Mendelson (in the *New Republic*, February 22, 1988) speaks of 'the office worker whose computer keystrokes are monitored by the central computer in the personnel office, and who will be fired if the keystrokes-per-minute figure doesn't match the corporate quota.' (Mr. Mendelson does not say what form of drudgery this worker is being saved from.)

And what are we to say of the diversely skilled country housewife who now bores the same six holes day after day on an assembly line? What higher form of womanhood or humanity is she evolving toward?

How, I am asking, can women improve themselves by submitting to the same specialization, degradation, trivialization, and tyrannization of work that men have submitted to? And that question is made legitimate by another: How have men improved themselves by submitting to it? The answer is that men have not, and women cannot, improve themselves by submitting to it.

Women have complained, justly, about the behavior of 'macho' men. But despite their he-man pretensions and their captivation by masculine heroes of sports, war, and the Old West, most men are now entirely accustomed to obeying and currying the favor of their bosses. Because of this, of course, they hate their jobs – they mutter, 'Thank God it's Friday' and 'Pretty good for Monday' – but they do as they are told. They are more compliant than most housewives have been. Their characters combine feudal submissiveness with modern helplessness. They have accepted almost without protest, and often with relief, their dispossession of any usable property and, with that, their loss of economic independence and their consequent subordination to bosses. They have submitted to the destruction of the household economy and thus of the household, to the loss of home employment and self-employment, to the disintegration of their families and communities, to the desecration and pillage of their country, and they have continued abjectly to believe, obey, and vote for the people who have most eagerly abetted this ruin and who have most profited from it. These men, moreover, are helpless to do anything for themselves or anyone else without money, and so for money they do whatever they are told. They know that their ability to be useful is precisely defined by their willingness to be somebody else's tool. Is it any wonder that they talk tough and worship athletes and cowboys? Is it any wonder that some of them are violent?

It is clear that women cannot justly be excluded from the daily fracas by which the industrial economy divides the spoils of society and nature, but their inclusion is a poor justice and no reason for applause. The enterprise is as devastating with women in it as it was before. There is no sign that women are exerting a 'civilizing influence' upon it. To have an equal part in our juggernaut of national vandalism is to be a vandal. To call this vandalism 'liberation' is to prolong, and even ratify, a dangerous confusion that was once principally masculine.

A broader, deeper criticism is necessary. The problem is not just the exploitation of women by men. A greater problem is that women and men alike are consenting to an economy that exploits women and men and everything else.

Another decent possibility my critics implicitly deny is that of work as a gift. Not one of them supposed that my wife may be a consulting engineer who helps me in her spare time out of the goodness of her heart; instead they suppose that she is 'a household drudge.' But what appears to infuriate them the most is their supposition that she works for nothing. They assume – and this is the orthodox assumption of the industrial economy – that the only help worth giving is not given at all, but sold. Love, friendship, neighborliness, compassion, duty – what are they? We are realists. We will be most happy to receive your check.

THE VARIOUS REDUCTIONS I have been describing are fairly directly the results of the ongoing revolution of applied science known as 'technological progress.' This revolution has provided the means by which both the productive and the consumptive capacities of people could be detached from household and community and made to serve other people's purely economic ends. It has provided as well a glamor of newness, ease, and affluence that made it seductive even to those who suffered most from it. In its more recent history especially, this revolution has been successful in putting unheard-of quantities of consumer goods and services within the reach of ordinary people. But the technical means of this popular 'affluence' has at the same time made possible the gathering of the real property and the real power of the country into fewer and fewer hands.

Some people would like to think that this long sequence of industrial innovations has changed human life and even human nature in fundamental ways. Perhaps it has – but, arguably, almost always for the worse. I know that 'technological progress' can be defended, but I observe that the defenses are invariably quantitative – catalogs of statistics on the ownership of automobiles and television sets, for example, or on the increase of life expectancy – and I see that these statistics are always kept carefully apart from the related statistics of soil loss, pollution, social disintegration, and so forth. That is to say, there is never an effort to determine the *net* result of this progress. The voice of its defenders is not that of the responsible bookkeeper, but that of the propagandist or salesman, who says that the net gain is more than 100 percent – that the thing we have bought has perfectly replaced everything it has cost, and added a great deal more: 'You just can't lose!' We thus have got rich by spending, just as the advertisers have told us we would, and the best of all possible worlds is getting better every day.

The statistics of life expectancy are favorites of the industrial apologists, because they are perhaps the hardest to argue with. Nevertheless, this emphasis on longevity is an excellent example of the way the isolated aims of the industrial mind reduce and distort human life, and also the way statistics corrupt the truth. A long life has indeed always been thought desirable; everything that is alive apparently wishes to continue to live. But until our own time, that sentence would have been qualified: long life is desirable and everything wishes to live *up to a point*. Past a certain point, and in certain conditions, death becomes preferable to life. Moreover, it was generally agreed that a good life was preferable to one that was merely long, and that the goodness of a life could not be determined by its length. The statisticians of longevity ignore good in both its senses; they do not ask if the prolonged life is virtuous, or if it is satisfactory. If the life is that of a vicious criminal, or if it is inched out in a veritable hell of captivity within the medical industry, no matter – both become statistics to 'prove' the good luck of living in our time.

But in general, apart from its own highly specialized standards of quantity and efficiency, 'technological progress' has produced a social and ecological decline. Industrial war, except by the most fanatically narrow standards, is worse than war used to be. Industrial agriculture, except by the standards of quantity and mechanical efficiency, diminishes everything it affects. Industrial workmanship is certainly worse than traditional workmanship, and is getting shoddier every day. After forty-odd years, the evidence is everywhere that television, far from proving a great tool of education, is a tool of stupefaction and disintegration. Industrial education has abandoned the old duty of passing on the cultural and intellectual inheritance in favor of baby-sitting and career preparation.

After several generations of 'technological progress,' in fact, we have become a people who *cannot* think about anything important. How far down in the natural order do we have to go to find creatures who raise their young as indifferently as industrial humans now do? Even the English sparrows do not let loose into the streets young sparrows who have no notion of their identity or their adult responsibilities. When else in history would you find 'educated' people who know more about sports than about the history of their country, or uneducated people who do not know the stories of their families and communities?

TO ASK A still more obvious question, what is the purpose of this technological progress? What higher aim do we think it is serving? Surely the aim cannot be the integrity or happiness of our families, which we have made subordinate to the education system, the television industry, and the consumer economy. Surely it cannot be the integrity or health of our communities, which we esteem even less than we esteem our families. Surely it cannot be love of our country, for we are far more concerned about the desecration of the flag than we are about the desecration of our land. Surely it cannot be the love of God, which counts for at least as little in the daily order of business as the love of family, community, and country.

The higher aims of 'technological progress' are money and ease. And this exalted greed for money and ease is disguised and justified by an obscure, cultish faith in 'the future.' We do as we do, we say, 'for the sake of the future' or 'to make a better future for our children.' How we can hope to make a good future by doing badly in the present, we do not say. We cannot think about the future, of course, for the future does not exist: the existence of the future is an article of faith. We can be assured only that, if there is to be a future, the good of it is already implicit in the good things of the present. We do not need to plan or devise a 'world of the future'; if we take care of the world of the present, the future will have received full justice from us. A good future is implicit in the soils, forests, grasslands, marshes, deserts, mountains, rivers, lakes, and oceans that we have now, and in the good things of human culture that we have now; the only valid 'futurology' available to us is to take care of those things. We have no need to contrive and dabble at 'the future of the human race'; we have the same pressing need that we have always had – to love, care for, and teach our children.

And so the question of the desirability of adopting any technological innovation is a question with two possible answers – not one, as has been commonly assumed. If one's motives are money, ease, and haste to arrive in a technologically determined future, then the answer is foregone, and there is, in fact, no question, and no thought. If one's motive is the love of family, community, country, and God, then one will have to think, and one may have to decide that the proposed innovation is undesirable.

The question of how to end or reduce dependence on some of the technological innovations already adopted is a baffling one. At least, it baffles me. I have not been able to see, for example, how people living in the country, where there is no public transportation, can give up their automobiles without becoming less useful to each other. And this is because, owing largely to the influence of the automobile, we live too far from each other, and from the things we need, to be able to get about by any other means. Of course, you *could* do without an automobile, but to do so you would have to disconnect yourself from many obligations. Nothing I have so far been able to think about this problem has satisfied me.

But if we have paid attention to the influence of the automobile on country communities, we know that the desirability of technological innovation is an issue that requires thinking about, and we should have acquired some ability to think about it. Thus if I am partly a writer, and I am offered an expensive machine to help me write, I ought to ask whether or not such a machine is desirable.

I should ask, in the first place, whether or not I wish to purchase a solution to a problem that I do not have. I acknowledge that, as a writer, I need a lot of help. And I have received an abundance of the best of help from my wife, from other members of my family, from friends, from teachers, from editors, and sometimes from readers. These people have helped me out of love or friendship, and perhaps in exchange for some help that I have given them. I suppose I should leave open the possibility that I need more help than I am getting, but I would certainly be ungrateful and greedy to think so.

But a computer, I am told, offers a kind of help that you can't get from other humans; a computer will help you to write faster, easier, and more. For a while, it seemed to me that every university professor I met told me this. Do I, then, want to write faster, easier, and more? No. My standards are not speed, ease, and quantity. I have already left behind too much evidence that, writing with a pencil, I have written too fast, too easily, and too much. I would like to be a *better* writer, and for that I need help from other humans, not a machine.

The professors who recommended speed, ease, and quantity to me were, of course, quoting the standards of their universities. The chief concern of the industrial system, which is to say the present university system, is to cheapen work by increasing volume. But implicit in the professors' recommendation was the idea that one needs to be up with the times. The pace-setting academic intellectuals have lately had a great hankering to be up with the times. They don't worry about keeping up with the Joneses: as intellectuals, they know that they are supposed to be Nonconformists and Independent Thinkers living at the Cutting Edge of Human Thought. And so they are all a-dither to keep up with the times – which means adopting the latest technological innovations as soon as the Joneses do.

Do I wish to keep up with the times? No.

MY WISH SIMPLY is to live my life as fully as I can. In both our work and our leisure, I think, we should be so employed. And in our time this means that we must save ourselves from the products that we are asked to buy in order, ultimately, to replace ourselves.

The danger most immediately to be feared in 'technological progress' is the degradation and obsolescence of the body. Implicit in the technological revolution from the beginning has been a new version of an old dualism, one always destructive, and now more destructive than ever. For many centuries there have been people who looked upon the body, as upon the natural world, as an encumbrance of the soul, and so have hated the body, as they have hated the natural world, and longed to be free of it. They have seen the body as intolerably imperfect by spiritual standards. More recently, since the beginning of the technological revolution, more and more people have looked upon the body, along with the rest of the natural creation, as intolerably imperfect by mechanical standards. They see

the body as an encumbrance of the mind –
the mind, that is, as reduced to a set of mechanical ideas that can be implemented in
machines – and so they hate it and long to
be free of it. The body has limits that the
machine does not have; therefore, remove
the body from the machine so that the machine can continue as an unlimited idea.

It is odd that simply because of its 'sexual freedom' our time should be considered
extraordinarily physical. In fact, our 'sexual revolution' is mostly an industrial phe-
nomenon, in which the body is used as an
idea of pleasure or a pleasure machine with
the aim of 'freeing' natural pleasure from
natural consequence. Like any other industrial enterprise, industrial sexuality seeks to
conquer nature by exploiting it and ignoring
the consequences, by denying any connec-
tion between nature and spirit or body and
soul, and by evading social responsibility.

The spiritual, physical, and economic costs of this 'freedom' are immense, and are characteristically belittled or ignored. The diseases of sexual irresponsibility are regarded as a technological problem and an affront to liberty. Industrial sex, characteristically, establishes its freeness and goodness by an industrial accounting, dutifully toting up numbers of 'sexual partners,' orgasms, and so on, with the inevitable industrial implication that the body is somehow a limit on the idea of sex, which will be a great deal more abundant as soon as it can be done by robots.

This hatred of the body and of the body's life in the natural world, always inherent in the technological revolution (and sometimes explicitly and vengefully so), is of concern to an artist because art, like sexual love, is of the body. Like sexual love, art is of the mind and spirit also, but it is made with the body and it appeals to the senses. To reduce or shortcut the intimacy of the body's involvement in the making of a work of art (that is, of any artifice, anything made by art) inevitably risks reducing the work of art and the art itself. In addition to the reasons I gave previously, which I still believe are good reasons, I am not going to use a computer because I don't want to diminish or distort my bodily involvement in my work. I don't want to deny myself the *pleasure* of bodily involvement in my work, for that pleasure seems to me to be the sign of an indispensable integrity.

At first glance, writing may seem not nearly so much an art of the body as, say, dancing or gardening or carpentry. And yet language is the most intimately physical of all the artistic means. We have it palpably in our mouths; it is our *langue*, our tongue. Writing it, we shape it with our hands. Reading aloud what we have written – as we must do, if we are writing carefully – our language passes in at the eyes, out at the mouth, in at the ears; the words are immersed and steeped in the senses of the body before they make sense in the mind. They *cannot* make sense in the mind until they have made sense in the body. Does shaping one's words with one's own hand impart character and quality to them, as does speaking them with one's own tongue to the satisfaction of one's own ear? There is no way to prove that it does. On the other hand, there is no way to prove that it does not, and I believe that it does.

The act of writing language down is not so insistently tangible an act as the act of building a house or playing the violin. But to the extent that it is tangible, I love the tangibility of it. The computer apologists, it seems to me, have greatly underrated the value of the handwritten manuscript as an artifact. I don't mean that a writer should be a fine calligrapher and write for exhibition, but rather that handwriting has a valuable influence on the work so written. I am certainly no calligrapher, but my handwritten pages have a homemade, handmade look to them that both pleases me in itself and suggests the possibility of ready correction. It looks hospitable to improvement. As the longhand is transformed into typescript and then into galley proofs and the printed page, it seems increasingly to resist improvement. More and more spunk is required to mar the clean, final-looking lines of type. I have the notion – again not provable – that the longer I keep a piece of work in longhand, the better it will be.

To me, also, there is a significant difference between ready correction and easy correction. Much is made of the ease of correction in computer work, owing to the insubstantiality of the light-image on the screen; one presses a button and the old version disappears, to be replaced by the new. But because of the substantiality of paper and the consequent difficulty involved, one does not handwrite or typewrite a new page every time a correction is made. A handwritten or typewritten page therefore is usually to some degree a palimpsest; it contains parts and relics of its own history – erasures, passages crossed out, interlineations – suggesting that there is something to go back to as well as something to go forward to. The light-text on the computer screen, by contrast, is an artifact typical of what can only be called the industrial present, a present absolute. A computer destroys the sense of historical succession, just as do other forms of mechanization. The well-crafted table or cabinet embodies the memory of (because it embodies respect for) the tree it was made of and the forest in which the tree stood. The work of certain potters embodies the memory that the clay was dug from the earth. Certain farms contain hospitably the remnants and reminders of the forest or prairie that preceded them. It is possible even for towns and cities to remember farms and forests or prairies. All good human work remembers its history. The best writing, even when printed, is full of intimations that it is the present version of earlier versions of itself, and that its maker inherited the work and the ways of earlier makers. It thus keeps, even in print, a suggestion of the quality of the handwritten page; it is a palimpsest.

Something of this undoubtedly carries over into industrial products. The plastic

Clorox jug has a shape and a loop for the forefinger that recalls the stoneware jug that went before it. But something vital is missing. It embodies no memory of its source or sources in the earth or of any human hand involved in its shaping. Or look at a large factory or a power plant or an airport, and see if you can imagine – even if you know – what was there before. In such things the materials of the world have entered a kind of orphanhood.

It would be uncharitable and foolish of me to suggest that nothing good will ever be written on a computer. Some of my best friends have computers. I have only said that a computer cannot help you to write *better*, and I stand by that. (In fact, I know a publisher who says that under the influence of computers – or of the immaculate copy that computers produce – many writers are now writing worse.) But I do say that in using computers writers are flirting with a radical separation of mind and body, the elimination of the work of the body from the work of the mind. The text on the computer screen, and the computer printout too, has a sterile, untouched, factorymade look, like that of a plastic whistle or a new car. The body does not do work like that. The body *characterizes* everything it touches. What it makes it traces over with the marks of its pulses and breathings, its excitements, hesitations, flaws, and mistakes. On its good work, it leaves the marks of skill, care, and love persisting through hesitations, flaws, and mistakes. And to those of us who love and honor the life of the body in this world, these marks are precious things, necessities of life.

But writing is of the body in yet another way. It is preeminently a walker's art. It can be done on foot and at large.

The beauty of its traditional equipment is simplicity. And cheapness. Going off to the woods, I take a pencil and some paper (*any* paper – a small notebook, an old envelope, a piece of a feed sack), and I am as well equipped for my work as the president of IBM. I am also free, for the time being at least, of everything that IBM is hooked to. My thoughts will not be coming to me from the power structure or the power grid, but from another direction and way entirely. My mind is free to go with my feet.

I know that there are some people, perhaps many, to whom you cannot appeal on behalf of the body. To them, disembodiment is a goal, and they long for the realm of pure mind – or pure machine; the difference is negligible. Their departure from their bodies, obviously, is much to be desired, but the rest of us had better be warned: they are going to cause a lot of dangerous commotion on their way out.

SOME OF MY critics were happy to say that my refusal to use a computer would not do any good. I have argued, and am convinced, that it will at least do *me* some good, and that it may involve me in the preservation of some cultural goods. But what they meant was real, practical, public good. They meant that the materials and energy I save by not buying a computer will not be 'significant.' They meant that no individual's restraint in the use of technology or energy will be 'significant.' That is true.

But each one of us, by 'insignificant' individual abuse of the world, contributes to a general abuse that is devastating. And if I were one of thousands or millions of people who could afford a piece of equipment, even one for which they had a conceivable 'need,' and yet did not buy it, *that* would be 'significant,' Why, then, should I hesitate for even a moment to be one, even the first one, of that 'significant' number? Thoreau gave the definitive reply to the folly of 'significant numbers' a long time ago: Why should anybody wait to do what is right until everybody does it? It is not 'significant' to love your own children or to eat your own dinner, either. But normal humans will not wait to love or eat until it is mandated by an act of Congress.

One of my correspondents asked where one is to draw the line. That question returns me to the bewilderment I mentioned earlier: I am unsure where the line ought to be drawn, or how to draw it. But it is an intelligent question, worth losing some sleep over.

I know how to draw the line only where it is easy to draw. It is easy – it is even a luxury – to deny oneself the use of a television set, and I zealously practice that form of self-denial. Every time I see television (at other people's houses), I am more inclined to congratulate myself on my deprivation. I have no doubt, as I have said, that I am better off without a computer. I joyfully deny myself a motorboat, a camping van, an off-road vehicle, and every other kind of recreational machinery. I have, and want, no 'second home.' I suffer very comfortably the lack of colas, TV dinners, and other counterfeit foods and beverages.

I am, however, still in bondage to the automobile industry and the energy companies, which have nothing to recommend them except our dependence on them. I still fly on airplanes, which have nothing to recommend them but speed; they are inconvenient, uncomfortable, undependable, ugly, stinky, and scary. I still cut my wood with a chainsaw, which has nothing to recommend it but speed, and has all the faults of an airplane, except it does not fly.

It is plain to me that the line ought to be drawn without fail wherever it can be drawn easily. And it ought to be easy (though many do not find it so) to refuse to buy what one does not need. If you are already solving your problem with the equipment you have – a pencil, say – why solve it with something more expensive and more damaging? If you don't have a problem, why pay for a solution? If you love the freedom and elegance of simple tools, why encumber yourself with something complicated?

And yet, if we are ever again to have a world fit and pleasant for little children, we are surely going to have to draw the line where it is *not* easily drawn. We are going to have to learn to give up things that we have learned (in only few years, after all) to 'need.' I am not an optimist; I am afraid that I won't live long enough to escape my bondage to the machines. Nevertheless, on every day left to me I will search my mind and circumstances for the means of escape. And I am not without hope. I knew a man who, in the age of chainsaws, went right on cutting his wood with a handsaw and an axe. He was a healthier and a saner man than I am. I shall let his memory trouble my thoughts.

(1989)

COUNTERPOINTS